THOM BARRETT

The STRENGTH *of* SURRENDER

A Chapbook of Heartfelt Poems

Copyright © 2024 by Thom Barrett.

All rights reserved. No part of this book may be reproduced or used in any manner without written permission of the copyright owner except for the use of quotations in a book review. For more information, contact: Info@livinglifewhiledying.com.

ISBN Hardcover: 979-8-9909823-6-9
ISBN Electronic: 979-8-9909823-5-2

Library of Congress Control Number: 2024926572

Publishing Consultant: PRESStinely, PRESStinely.com

Portions of this book are works of nonfiction. Certain names and identifying characteristics have been changed.

Printed in the United States of America.

Thom Barrett
Living Life Press
www.livinglifewhiledying.com

Disclaimer:

The resources in this book are provided for informational purposes only. They should not be used to replace the specialized training and professional judgment of a health care or mental health care professional.

*To those traveling the difficult road,
navigating the weight of uncertainty, pain, and change—
This book is for you.
May you find solace in the strength of surrender,
hope in the act of letting go,
and courage to embrace acceptance,
even when the path seems impassable.*

You are not alone.

Preface

My Journey of Acceptance

Life takes us on journeys we never anticipated—through places we've longed to visit, experiences that shape us, and inner landscapes we didn't even know existed. This chapbook is a collection of moments from my travels, not just the ones that led me through mountains and forests. These poems reflect the many forms of acceptance life has asked of me: accepting myself, help from others, loss, change, and, most importantly, the realization that joy is a choice we can make, even in the shadow of adversity, sorrow, and grief.

Perhaps the most challenging form of acceptance has been making peace with my own mortality. Some of the poems in this collection reflect the raw truth of living with an uncertain future, but they also show the resilience that blooms when I choose not just to survive but to live fully. For a long time, I feared falling asleep at night, worried I wouldn't wake up. I realized I wasn't afraid of death itself but of leaving too soon, wondering if I'd done enough to guide my daughters to leave behind a legacy of love and strength. Confronting that fear taught me that strength isn't just about clinging to life; it's about using the time I have to create something meaningful to leave a mark.

Choosing the themes of acceptance and joy felt natural for this collection. The last ten years of my life have been marked by lessons I never expected. I've faced heart disease, a painful divorce, a traumatic brain injury, and, perhaps most daunting of all, a diagnosis of stage IV, incurable prostate cancer. That moment shook me in a way nothing else had. For a long time, I was in turmoil, struggling to process my new reality. But eventually, I understood that while I couldn't control my diagnosis, I could control my response to it. Acceptance wasn't surrender—it was an active choice to live as fully as possible. And joy, I learned, was also a choice.

Emotions like sorrow, grief, anger, and even happiness are often reactions to life's events. But joy is different. Joy isn't dependent on circumstances; it's a conscious decision to seek the light, even in shadowed places. This understanding changed everything: I could hold joy and sorrow in the same space. Joy became an anchor, a way to stay grounded when life felt chaotic.

These challenges taught me that acceptance isn't passive; it's something I practice daily. It often begins with the problematic—losses, changes, or uncertainties—but over time, it reveals something more profound: that even in hardship, I still have choices. I can choose to recognize and embrace what is good, even when it's hard to see. This practice has become as natural as breathing.

Finding Joy in the Struggle

One night, I sat in a small bar in Ushuaia, the southernmost city in the world, surrounded by travelers carrying their own stories of adventure and trial. As I looked out over the vast, cold waters of the Beagle Channel, I thought about the long journey that had brought me there—not just in miles, but in resilience and quiet realizations. That night, I understood that acceptance is not a single destination but a practice woven through the challenges we face. It's found in fighting, grieving, and in the moments when joy is chosen, soft but unshakeable.

Growing older has also taught me that acceptance isn't always about pushing through to the next peak. Sometimes, it's about slowing down enough to savor the present. In "Embracing Change," I reflect on the shift from the relentless explorer of my younger years to someone who finds joy in a quieter pace. The body changes, but the spirit's hunger for life remains, and there's a new strength in learning to be at peace with exactly where I am.

I was reminded of this lesson on a recent hike at Iguazu Falls in Brazil. The heat and fatigue caught up with me, forcing frequent stops. Strangers offered me water, which I instinctively refused. It wasn't until someone quietly set a water bottle beside me that I realized how reluctant I was to accept help. That moment showed me that acceptance wasn't just about facing illness or aging; it was about allowing others in and recognizing that sometimes strength is found in accepting kindness. And in that acceptance, I found joy, even in the struggle.

Connection is another theme woven through this chapbook. In "In the Shadows of Struggle," I write about the love and support that sustain us. I've learned that while independence is admirable, true strength often comes when we allow others to share in our journey. It's in whispered words, a gentle touch, and shared moments that we find courage and joy.

Finding Joy in the Simple Moments

Acceptance isn't just surrendering to life's difficulties; it's celebrating its beauty. Even with a terminal diagnosis, there is room for laughter, wonder, and joy. Watching a starry night in Wyoming, where shooting stars light up the sky, or standing beneath the glow of a full moon reminds me that life is meant to be savored. Choosing to see and accept those moments is an act of strength, a way of choosing joy.

Nature has been my guide and companion throughout this journey. Whether it's the vast Alaskan wilderness of "Alaskan Road Warrior: Winter's Prelude" or the plains and mountains of Canada in *"Canadian Tapestry,: A Journey's Melody"* the land has taught me about resilience, solitude, and peace. The poems about my travels aren't just stories of where I've been; they're lessons about the joy found in the simplest moments.

These poems take you into the silence of snow-covered fields, moments of solitude that reveal life's fragile beauty, and the hope that comes from connecting with others. I've walked snowy mountain passes, felt the bite of the Antarctic wind, and stood in awe as dawn broke over new horizons. These experiences taught me the true meaning of strength and acceptance, shaping who I am today.

Each poem in this chapbook is part of the larger journey of acceptance and joy. As you read, I hope you find not just my story but echoes of your own. These poems were my way of making sense of life's twists and turns, but I hope they remind you that we're all on this path together. I hope you find pieces of your own story reflected in my poems. I hope they remind you of the moments when you've had to accept, let go, or find joy in the quiet spaces between life's more significant events.

Acceptance is active and brave—a choice to see life's beauty and hardship and to keep walking forward with an open heart. It takes many forms. Sometimes it's a quiet nod, and other times it's an uphill battle. But through it all, joy can be a companion, a choice that lights the way. Wherever you are in your journey, I hope these pages remind you that acceptance and joy are both acts of courage.

Welcome. May you find comfort and moments of your own acceptance within these words.

—Thom Barrett

Table of Contents

Preface .... **v**
   My Journey of Acceptance v
      Finding Joy in the Struggle vi
      Finding Joy in the Simple Moments vii
Table of Contents .... **ix**
   Acceptance of Self-Reflection 1
      Who I Have Become 2
      In the Heart of a Dreamer 3
   Acceptance of Support 4
      In the Shadow of Struggle 5
      Canadian Tapestry: A Journey's Melody 6
   Acceptance of Emotional Responses 7
      Reflections in the Night 8
      Acceptance Isn't Surrender 9
   Acceptance of Loss and Limitations 10
      Embracing Change 11
   Acceptance of Change and Transformation 13
      The Measure of Time 14
      In the Light 16
   Acceptance of Adversity 17
      The Inescapable Weight of Sorrow and Misery 18
      Winter Cowboy: Today's Trail 20
   Acceptance of Uncertainty 21
      Alaskan Road Warrior: Winter's Prelude 22
      I Wonder if I'm Going Mad 23
   Acceptance of Mortality 24
      Why I Travel with Terminal Cancer 25
   Freedom in Acceptance 27
      Freedom's Path 27

Conclusion	31
Freedom Within Acceptance	33
A Note of Gratitude	34
Acknowledgments	35
About the Author	37

Acceptance of Self-Reflection

Personal discovery was the first step on this journey of acceptance. Before I could embrace life's challenges, I needed to understand who I was and where I was headed. It's about looking inward, confronting the truths that shape us, and acknowledging our strengths and vulnerabilities. For me, this journey began with moments of deep introspection—questioning my choices, my dreams, and what it meant to stay true to myself in the face of adversity.

These poems reflect the highs and lows of that journey. "Who I Have Become" was born during a time when doubt threatened to consume me—a dark period where I felt lost and uncertain about everything. What stopped me from spiraling into despair was the conscious choice to pause, reflect, and look for the light, even in the smallest forms. I realized that self-reflection isn't just about facing the darkness; it's about actively seeking the strength to move forward. That decision became the heart of this poem—a reminder that within the struggle lies the power to redefine ourselves.

"In the Heart of a Dreamer" came from a very different moment: the thrill of doing something I love—planning a trip. But this wasn't just any trip; it was an epic seven-month road journey across Canada and the US, from the far reaches of Fairbanks, Alaska, to the red rocks of Moab, Utah—all in the depths of winter. For me, this trip symbolized more than just travel—it was about reclaiming a sense of adventure and daring to dream again. It reminded me that even when life feels unpredictable, there's always beauty to be found in the act of moving forward.

Through these poems, I explore the duality of light and darkness, of doubt and hope, and struggle and discovery. They represent the moments that shaped me, and I hope they inspire you to reflect on your own journey.

The Strength of Surrender

In "Who I Have Become," I explore the process of realizing that I am more than just the sum of my achievements or the miles I've traveled. This poem represents that turning point where I started to accept myself as a whole person, complete with imperfections and strengths. It's about understanding that the journey inward is as vital as any outward adventure.

Who I Have Become

Not just the sum of miles I've roamed,
Or the countless paths that I've called home.
I'm more than what these hands have done,
More than battles lost or won.

I've touched hearts and felt them in return,
In every hug, in every lesson learned.
Connections made, not by blood alone,
But by souls who've helped me feel less alone.

I stand, not just for me but for those,
Who find strength in the way my story goes.
Not just for loved ones but strangers, too,
Who see in my fight what they might do.

I am an explorer of worlds unseen,
Of minds, emotions, and all between.
I chart the seas of thought and heart,
Where human connection plays its part.

The hugs I've received, the hands I've held,
Have shaped the person I've become, compelled.
To journey deeper, beyond just land,
To where the spirit seeks to understand.

Who I've become is still a work in progress,
A soul forever striving, learning, blessed.
There's so much more yet to unfold,
In a story still daring, still bold.

I am the hearts I've touched, the love I've known,
The living proof that none of us stand alone.

An explorer, yes—of earth and sky,
But also of the bonds that tie.

And who I've become is far from done,
With so much more still to become.

Thom Barrett

In "In the Heart of a Dreamer" captures the excitement and anticipation of a journey that moves through the different seasons—each representing a new chapter of experiences. The poem reflects how I find joy in the process of exploring and adapting to what comes, understanding that change is part of life's adventure. It shows that transformation happens not just in grand moments but in the smaller memories and experiences that shape me over time.

In the Heart of a Dreamer

In the heart of a dreamer, a journey takes shape,
A grand expedition, an escape.
Across North America's vast domain,
From sunlit beaches to misty plains.

Maps sprawl across the table wide,
Marking a path for the long, joyous ride.
Fall's tapestry in the East unfolds,
Winter's majesty in the North holds.

Each point on the map, a story to tell,
Of cities, forests, where spirits dwell.
A thrill for vistas yet unseen,
From azure coasts to valleys green.

Planning for seasons, a dance of time,
Fall's leafy trails, winter's frosty climb.
Spring's bloom waits in the journey's wake,
Each phase a new memory to make.

The gear is gathered, each detail keen,
For trekking, skiing, and places in between.
The excitement of cultures, people to meet,
From bustling cities to quiet retreats.

With each step, a discovery anew,
Of oneself, of the world, in a view.
A tapestry of travel, rich and vast,
In each moment, memories are cast.

Adventures planned under autumn's moon,
Departure awaits; it can't come too soon.
The road calls out an endless allure,
Each mile reveals life's essence pure.

Acceptance of Support

Acceptance is not something we achieve alone. It's built upon the connections and communities that sustain us when life becomes difficult. Leaning on others, sharing our stories, and feeling the support of those who care for us helps to lighten the load and remind us that we are not alone in our struggles. This stage of the journey emphasizes the power of shared understanding and collective resilience.

Thanks to my friends who understand the importance of connection better than I ever did. Their texts checking in or voicemails sharing their own moments remind me that I am not just a person navigating challenges but someone who is seen, valued, and loved. These simple acts make me feel "normal" and connected in ways I never expected.

One evening, when I felt particularly lost, a friend's simple message, "Brother T, your silence has me worried. You OK?" reminded me that I wasn't alone. I've learned that true connection isn't just received—it's shared. And in sharing, we find the strength to keep moving forward, even when the road is difficult.

Thom Barrett

In "In the Shadows of Struggle," I write about how the love and support from friends and family became a lifeline during moments of despair. This poem reflects the importance of allowing ourselves to be vulnerable, to accept the care of others, and to see that strength is often found not just within but in those around us.

In the Shadow of Struggle

In the shadows where the weary tread,
Fatigue raises its unwanted head.
It's not the tiredness of a long day's end,
But a constant weight no sleep can mend.

Once a builder with projects galore,
Now, simple tasks become a chore.
A teen's vigor, now memories distant,
Each move met with pain and resistance.

Naps, once foreign, now a daily delight,
Resting anywhere within sight.
Nausea whispers, a relentless blight,
Brain fog steals the mind's clear sight.

With ruler in hand, I pause and forget,
Memory loss is a constant threat.
Measurements fade, steps retraced,
The plan, the design, is perpetually misplaced.

Conversations falter, words escape,
A story half-told, waiting to take shape.
Hot flashes strike; in cold, they burn,
Steamed glasses a constant concern.

Sweat-soaked nights, sleep's fragile thread,
Tossing, turning in a restless bed.
Emotions swing, a pendulum wide,
A storm within, no place to hide.

Through all these trials, a soul laid bare,
Hope emerges in the love we share.
Friends and family, a steadfast crew,
Their strength and comfort ever true.

In moments dark, when spirits fade,
Their light surrounds, fears allayed.
Through whispered words and gentle touch,
They remind me I am loved so much.

Though cancer's grip and treatments drain,
In their presence, I find strength again.
With every hug, each hand held tight,
They are my solace in the night.

So, in the shadows where I roam,
I find my way—I am not alone.
For love and care, a saving grace,
In their embrace, I find my place.

This poem, "Canadian Tapestry," reminds me that transformation isn't just found in the grand, sweeping views but also in the people and moments that touch us along the way. It's about welcoming change and finding meaning in the collective experiences that shape who we become.

Canadian Tapestry: A Journey's Melody

From East to West, a journey's call,
In Canada's embrace, we find our all.
First, Ontario's waters clear,
With lakes and falls that draw us near.

In every ripple, a story's told,
Along these shores, where tales unfold.
Niagara's thunder, a mighty sound,
In its spray, our spirits bound.

Onto the prairies, fields of gold,
Where skies and lands in beauty hold.
A vastness so profound, so pure,
In these open arms, we feel secure.

The horizon meets the traveler's gaze,
In wheat-sea fields, where one could laze.
The sun sets in a prairie fire,
Painting scenes that never tire.

Then rise the mountains, peaks so high,
Their majesty piercing the sky.
The Rockies stand in regal grace,
In their shadows, our hearts race.

Snow-capped guardians of the land,
Beneath them, our petty worries stand.
Each vista steals our breath in awe,
In their presence, we find our law.

But more than scenes, it's people's grace,
That makes this land a welcoming place.
In every town, a friendly face,
In Canada, we find our place.

Acceptance of Emotional Responses

Emotional responses are an essential part of being human, and both acceptance and surrender are deeply intertwined with how we navigate these emotions. One of the first steps in the journey of acceptance is learning to allow ourselves to feel—whether it's sorrow, happiness, anger, or fear—without judgment. Emotions are not something we can always control, but accepting them is crucial for moving forward.

Surrendering, however, is about giving up hope in the face of these emotions. It's allowing fear or sorrow to dictate our actions, letting anger paralyze us, or losing ourselves to despair. Surrender happens when we let emotions overwhelm us, refusing to see beyond the momentary storm.

Acceptance, in contrast, is about holding space for these feelings, recognizing that they are natural, temporary, and ultimately do not define us. It's about engaging with emotions, not as something to fight or succumb to, but as a part of our journey toward understanding and growth. To accept is to face emotions with courage and clarity, keep hope alive even in the darkest moments, and move forward with intention.

There was a period when I could not find sleep; each day, the weight of the world pressed down on me, making it harder to move. By refusing to accept my initial thoughts of fear at face value, I was able to probe deeper and uncover what truly frightened me—love and legacy. This deeper understanding transformed my perspective, revealing that fear often masks what we value most. It is now an essential part of each day—showing love to those around me and leaving a legacy through the moments I share with them. This process taught me that understanding and accepting my emotional responses is not a one-time event but an ongoing practice that shapes how I live each day.

In "Reflections in the Night," I share the raw emotions that arise when facing my deepest fears and worries. The poem takes an honest look at the nights spent wrestling with doubt and concern, highlighting how acceptance begins by acknowledging those feelings without resistance.

Reflections in the Night

I never thought I'd fear the night,
Or closing my eyes against the light.
What was once a welcome rest,
Now summons battles in my chest.

What if sleep, so soft and deep,
Becomes the last I'll ever keep?
The last embrace, the final sigh,
The warmth of my dog at my feet, nearby.

It's not just the dark that stirs me so;
It's questions that, in the silence, grow.
Not missed goals or undone quests—
It's love that weighs upon my chest.

Have I done enough to leave my mark,
A guiding light when days turn dark?
Will the love I gave, the stories shared,
Be strong enough when life feels unfair?

My body, once strong, now distant and strange,
Each day is a reminder of this change.

I've fought to accept what I cannot mend,
Resistance steals more than it can defend.

And yet, despite all I've come to know,
The fear is not in death's shadowed glow.
It's the legacy, the love I give—
Will it be enough for them to live?

I lie awake, heart heavy, eyes wide,
Wondering if I've left behind,
A map, a guide, a steady flame—
Something more than just a name.

This is hard, overwhelming too,
But in the quiet, I feel what's true:
The most vital moments come and go,
Shared in whispers, soft and slow.

To choose joy, even as shadows loom,
To face the fear in the dim-lit room.
Not just in strength, but in love's embrace—
The gift I'll leave, my lasting trace.

This poem, "Acceptance Isn't Surrender," is a declaration of strength and resilience in the face of life's hardest truths. For me, it's about rejecting the idea of giving up or being defined by my challenges. Surrender feels like letting hope and action slip away—something I refuse to do.

Instead, acceptance is an act of courage. It's about facing reality without denial or avoidance, embracing what it is while finding purpose, joy, and the power to move forward. This poem reminds me that while I can't control everything, I can control my response. It's a testament to living fully, intentionally, and authentically, even in the face of an ongoing fight.

Acceptance Isn't Surrender

For me, acceptance is not surrender,
It is the spark, the steady ember.
Surrender folds, admits defeat,
Lays down the will, concedes retreat.

To surrender is to let hope go,
To stop the fight, let shadows grow.
It leaves no room for change or action,
No space for growth or satisfaction.

But that's not me, it's not my way,
I choose to meet each daunting day.
Acceptance stands where fear might cower,
An act of grace, a quiet power.

I see the truth, this insidious fight,
An incurable foe in the dimmest light.
Yet I won't deny, ignore, or flee,
This is my reality, it's part of me.

Acceptance speaks, "I face the storm,
Not passively, but to transform."
To know what is, not wish it gone,
To meet the dusk, to greet the dawn.

It clears the path for what can be,
A chance to act, to live, to see.
It frees the heart, removes the weight,
Aligns the soul to choose its fate.

It's not defeat, it's choosing how,
To shape the life I'm living now.
To channel strength, to rise, to cope,
To seek out joy, to build on hope.

Acceptance whispers, "You are free,
To shape your life, your destiny."
And though the fight may still persist,
My will to live will not be missed.

Acceptance of Loss and Limitations

Accepting our limitations is one of the more challenging aspects of acceptance. Whether it's the constraints imposed by aging, health, or circumstances beyond our control, recognizing that we cannot do everything we once could is difficult but necessary. This stage of the journey is about making peace with what we can no longer change and learning to adapt to our new realities.

There was one particular trek we were on in Torres del Paine where I couldn't go any further and opted to stay back while the others continued. It was to be a three-hour wait for them to return, and during that time, I fought through a storm of emotions—from anger at myself to a deeper understanding that this was another crossroad on the journey of acceptance. As I sat there alone, watching the clouds shift over the jagged peaks and feeling the wind on my face, I began to realize that this moment had its own value, even if it wasn't what I had originally planned. Limitations are real, and I needed to accept them if I was going to live this life as fully as I could. I had to understand that there are different ways to find joy in where I am and what I can do, even if it looks different from what I imagined.

This realization became a reminder that life is not measured by how far we go but by how deeply we engage with the moments we're given, even if they are spent sitting quietly on the sidelines.

In "Embracing Change," I recount my transition from the relentless explorer who never paused to the man who has learned to move at a slower, more reflective pace. This poem embodies the shift from resistance to acceptance, showing that while our bodies may change, our spirits can still remain strong.

Embracing Change

As I sit with time's quiet toll,
I feel its pull on my heart and soul.
Life around me hums so bright,
Yet inside is a quieter fight.

It's not the restlessness of youth,
But grappling with a harder truth—
The man I was, so bold and free,
Now, meets the man I've come to be.

Once, I sought the highest peaks,
The thrill of risk, the wild's mystique.
Skiing steep slopes from side to side,
Believing strength was mine to ride.

But now, each creak, each aching bend,
Reminds me that those days must end.
No longer quick to leap or run,
I weigh my limits one by one.

It's easy to mourn the loss of might,
To miss the man who climbed with light.
But here's the truth I've come to see:
Life's not the same, but it's still free.

For strength, I've learned, is more than bone,
It's found in what we call our own—
The will to rise, the heart to stay,
To greet the dawn of each new day.

My body now is marked with change,
Yet, through these shifts, I've rearranged.
What once I thought was fixed, unbent—
And made my peace with what it meant.

The Strength of Surrender

The thrill of life's no longer fast,
But found in moments meant to last—
A sunset's glow, a simple walk,
A cherished friend with whom to talk.

The me of youth still holds my hand,
But now I understand the land,
Of limits, of slowing pace,
Of finding joy in a gentler race.

Strength is not just found in might,
But in the soul's enduring fight—
To adapt, accept, and persevere,
Even when the path's unclear.

I've seen the world from mountaintops,
But now I pause before I hop.
I used to scoff at slower ways,
But now I honor measured days.

For life's not bound by miles or speed—
But by the depth of what we heed.
Each new phase, though different still,
Is part of the journey, part of the thrill.

And so I stand on changing ground,
With lessons learned, with wisdom found.

My battles now are not with height,
But with accepting where I fight.

I'll seek the Arctic's polar light,
Or the Rockies' towering, snow-capped might.
And if I can't climb to the top,
I'll find a chairlift and take the drop.

No obstacle shall block my path,
For where there's will, I'll find the craft.
The view is worth this different way,
The journey holds its quiet sway.

For in the stillness, strength I find,
In this evolving state of mind.
For life's adventure isn't speed,
But in the moments that we feed.

And so I'll go, in steps or slow,
Embracing each new place I grow.
For I am more than skin and bone—
My spirit's strength is all my own.

This journey's changed, but still it's mine—
I'll seek, I'll thrive, in all I find.
For, in the end, it's not how fast,
But how we live and make it last.

Acceptance of Change and Transformation

Change and transformation are constants in life. Accepting them requires letting go of who we are and embracing who we are becoming. This stage of the journey is about recognizing that life's shifts—whether planned or unexpected—reshape us and that transformation is part of growth.

Do people transform because they need to or because they choose to? Have I transformed because of this illness or because I wanted to feel empowered in the midst of what this disease was taking away from me? I realized that while this illness forced me to change, I had the power to choose how I responded to it. I chose to take the positive path—to take control of my life and make changes that align with what I needed and the quality of life I wanted to have. This journey taught me that while life's trials may push us to transform, it's the choices we make within those moments that define who we become

In "The Measure of Time," I reflect on the inevitability of change and how it alters our perception of life. It is a meditation on the passage of time and the acceptance that each phase brings new lessons, perspectives, and new versions of ourselves.

The Measure of Time

In the waning hours of a borrowed dawn,
Time whispers softly, a fleeting song.
Once boundless and vast, now a precious thread,
Spun from the moments that lie ahead.

Where once it stretched as far as you could see,
Now counts each breath with stark urgency.
A river that once roared wild and free,
Flows gently toward the end's decree.

Shall I stand as witness on the shore?
Or dive into the current once more?
Shall I craft worlds from the sands of time,
Or walk the paths that others have lined?

Shall I read and dream beneath fading light,
Or pen tales that illuminate the night?
Shall I follow trails where others trod,
Or blaze a path, a testament to living fully.

When sunset paints the sky with fire,
Is it enough to simply admire?
Or do I capture the fleeting light,
Crafting dawn from the depths of night?

Shall my days be counted by the suns I greet,
Or by the hearts that in my presence beat?
Do I count the embraces, tender and mild,
Or the laughter shared, the tears beguiled?

Is there a measure true for time so thin?
Not in the breadth, but the depth within—
The quiet strength of surrender's grin,
A peace found deep beneath the din.

Thom Barrett

A creator of moments, a seeker of light,
Turning the pages where my passions write.
Each tick a purpose, each tock a song,
In the finite dance where my days belong.

Let time be measured in love and deeds,
In the pursuit of dreams, in planting seeds.
As twilight lengthens, shadows cast,
I find peace in each moment passed.

To witness, to create, to touch, to be,
In each counted second, I am finally free.
As time's sands slip, I embrace each grain—
A life well-loved, embraced by all.

"In the Light" explores my ability to appreciate the beauty and purpose in both beginnings and endings, recognizing that transformation isn't only found in monumental moments but in the daily cycles that encourage presence and gratitude.

In essence, this poem serves as a personal reminder that true acceptance comes from recognizing and appreciating each phase of life. It shows me that change is not just something to endure but something that holds its own beauty and significance. This poem invites me—and others—to find solace and fulfillment in the rhythm of change and to embrace each moment as it arrives.

In the Light

I often wonder about the light—
And how morning and afternoon glow differently.
Where I live, I love the sunrise,
amber streaming through the trees,
a warmth beyond mere sight—
it's comfort, an invitation.

Perhaps it's the darkness left behind,
that makes the light a welcome friend,
a signal of hope,
a whisper of renewal.

For me, sunrise is gratitude—
the gift of another day,
a well of strength to draw from,
as I face what's yet to come.

But sunset is something else—
a clarity of a different kind.

The light, sharper, cleaner,
wraps the day in calm,
a quiet sigh of closure,
as evening gently steps in.

It's a time to pause, to be still,
thankful for the chance to witness,
all that unfolded,
for the moments I've been given—
the smiles, the hugs,
the simple joys I've carried with me.

In that fading light, I feel present,
rooted in the day that was,
content with all its gifts,
and ready to release it,
as night draws near.

Acceptance of Adversity

Adversity is a reality we all face, but accepting it as part of life's fabric can be transformative. It doesn't mean surrendering to hardship but rather understanding that resilience and growth often come from facing difficult times head-on. This phase of acceptance acknowledges that suffering exists, but so does our capacity to endure and find meaning within it.

I have found adversity has a way of shaping us in unexpected ways. I have been on so many travels – not all of them joyful and full of positivity. Some travels were arduous, and some ended in injury and failure. Over time, I have determined that there are four levels of fun, which range from the lighthearted to the profoundly transformative.

- **Level 1:** Immediate fun, where joy and laughter are experienced in the moment. These rare flashes of light sustain us through dark times, even if they're just shared smiles or a brief reprieve from struggle.

- **Level 2:** The delayed sense of achievement that comes after pushing through challenges. You may feel exhausted during the climb, but the view from the summit brings a sense of accomplishment that makes the effort worthwhile. In facing adversity, these are the moments when resilience pays off, even if only recognized afterward.

- **Level 3:** The kind of "fun" that's disguised as struggle. At the time, it feels anything but enjoyable and may take weeks, months, or even years to appreciate. Only later do you realize the journey itself—the lessons learned and the growth achieved—was the true reward.

- **Level 4:** The experiences that were never fun and never will be but become meaningful over time. These are the moments where joy is absent, replaced instead by resilience and survival. They are the stories we carry as proof of endurance, learning, and inner strength.

In my journey, I've experienced all four levels. While Level 1 moments bring joy, the most lasting lessons come from Levels 3 and 4. These experiences were when I thought I might break but didn't, and the understanding that while joy can be a choice, growth is often a necessity. Adversity takes us through these levels, showing us that life is not just about immediate happiness but about finding meaning in the moments that challenge us the most.

"The Inescapable Weight of Sorrow and Misery" delves into the heavy emotional toll that comes with facing a terminal illness. This poem is raw and honest, capturing the struggle of accepting adversity and the journey toward finding peace in the midst of it.

The Inescapable Weight of Sorrow and Misery

When the news came, it ripped me apart,
Stage IV, incurable—an arrow to the heart.
I thought I was winning, beating the tide,
But the battle was lost; all hope had died.

I'd roamed for months, the wild calling my name,
Hiking, skiing, chasing freedom's flame.
I felt strong; I felt whole, invincible, and free—
Only to realize cancer had taken hold of me.

A routine visit, a seismic shift,
I felt like I was being pushed off a cliff.
The words hit hard, metastasized, and spread,
A broken road where hope had fled.

My body, as if it too now knew,
Released its hold, letting fatigue breakthrough.
Nausea, breathlessness, pain all around,
Symptoms appeared as if they'd been found.

Sorrow settled in, a deep, endless ache,
A place I stayed, afraid to wake.
To a reality barren and stark,
Where hope was lost in the dark.

There, in that sorrow, I found a hollow shield,
To guard against false hopes and trials revealed.

Thom Barrett

For I had been down this road before,
Only to find it had grown once more.

Yet in that darkness, moments arose,
A sunbeam's warmth, a petal's close.
A friend's laughter breaks the silence apart,
Reminders that life still held art.

Happiness, fleeting, reactionary and thin,
Came and went like an uninvited kin.
And anger—I felt its fierce, raw power,
A brief relief in a desperate hour.

But joy, I learned, was a different fight,
A conscious reach for a softer light.
A practice, not fleeting, rooted deep,
A choice to make, a promise to keep.

I looked for it in the smallest things—
The rustle of leaves, the flap of wings.
Moments that didn't demand or shout,
But whispered, "Life's still here, don't doubt."

Acceptance grew not in one grand sweep,
But in tiny steps, from shallow to deep.
Not just of pain or the body's decline,
But of the love that continues to shine.

What I feared wasn't death's cold claim,
But if I'd done enough, left more than a name.
Would my daughters know how to live,
Did I offer them all I had to give?

In that sleepless battle, eyes open wide,
I found an answer I couldn't hide.
Acceptance isn't a final defeat,
It's choosing joy, finding peace where fears meet.

The weight remains, but so does the light,
A balance of sorrow and joy each night.
To live, to love, to let both be—
This is the journey; this is me.

The Strength of Surrender

In "Winter Cowboy: Today's Trail," we follow a modern cowboy who embodies the spirit of confronting life's hardships head-on. With a snow-dusted hat and a pickup as his steed, he rides through the unforgiving landscape of a winter's night, symbolizing the determination and willpower needed to face the long and challenging road.

The poem shows that acceptance of adversity is not just about surviving but carrying forward with purpose, even when the path is fraught with challenges. It's about finding that fire within to continue moving, no matter how daunting the journey may be.

Winter Cowboy: Today's Trail

In lands where winter whispers white,
A cowboy rides as day meets night.
Not of old, with lasso and steed,
But a modern soul, where old paths lead.

His hat, snow-dusted, shades his eyes,
Against the glare of vast, cold skies.
His horse, a pickup, rugged, strong,
Carries him where the days are long.

The prairies vast, now fields of frost,
Echo the tales of the lost.
Yet in his heart, the fire burns bright,
Guiding him through the longest night.

With memories of past trails in his veins,
He rides on despite life's refrains.
Through snowflakes that dance in the chill,
He upholds the cowboy's timeless will.

A symbol of grit in the modern age,
A living chapter, not confined to a page.
His journey under the winter moon,
Sings a tune of a resilient croon.

The spirit of the West, forever alive,
As the winter cowboy rides, fierce and alive.

Acceptance of Uncertainty

Uncertainty is a part of life that few find easy to accept. It's the unknowns that often keep us up at night, filling us with worry. Reaching a point where we can accept uncertainty means acknowledging that not everything is within our control and learning to move forward despite it.

Uncertainty and I have had a running dialogue for oh-so long. In my previous life, my job was about minimizing uncertainty, reducing risks, and finding ways to control the backlash when uncertainty struck. The gift that this disease has provided me is the realization that I cannot control everything and that I need to live with and alongside uncertainty. Embracing this has taught me to find peace in the unknown and appreciate the present moment. In letting go of the need for control, I've learned that life's most profound lessons often come from what we can't predict or plan for.

The Strength of Surrender

"Alaskan Road Warrior: Winter's Prelude" speaks to the unpredictability of a journey into the unknown. The poem is a metaphor for the road of life, which twists and turns without guarantees. It represents the courage it takes to keep going, even when the future is unclear.

Alaskan Road Warrior: Winter's Prelude

In the land where the Northern Lights play,
A road warrior finds his way.
Through the vast, untamed Alaskan wild,
Nature's rugged, unspoiled child.

His steed, a truck of steel and might,
Cuts through the day and into the night.
Mountains loom like silent giants,
In this realm, he rides, self-reliant.

The road, a ribbon through the trees,
Twists and turns with the greatest ease.
Each mile, a new discovery,
Alaska's heart, vast and free.

As winter whispers in the air,
The landscape dons a snowy flare.
He drives through towns, sparse and small,
Where the spirit of the frontier stands tall.

The oncoming cold, a daunting guest,
Puts the road warrior to the test.
Yet, in this challenge, he finds his peace,
In the wilderness, all worries cease.

Through the taiga, over streams,
His journey like a waking dream.
The Northern Lights, a guiding blaze,
Illuminate his path through endless days.

In this journey, there's a truth he's found,
In the wild, where life abounds.
With every mile, doubt fades away,
As he embraces each fleeting day.

The road warrior, in his quest,
Finds freedom in each moment's crest.

"I Wonder if I'm Going Mad" dives into my restless thoughts and existential questions about life, identity, and transformation. By questioning my place within the cycle of life, I embody the struggle to understand my purpose and direction amidst the unknown. This reflective piece invites me and others to find peace in the questions themselves and to recognize that life's meaning often lies in the search, not just the answers.

I Wonder if I'm Going Mad

I wonder if I am going mad.
I cannot sleep, my mind won't rest,
As if I'm failing life's final test.

All I do is think—of birth, decay,
Growth and rebirth, life's cyclic way.
Where do I fit? What phase am I in?

I live more in my mind these days,
Than in the places I should tread.

Thoughts of consciousness fill my head—
How can I stretch it, expand it,
Before the light begins to fade?

How to go beyond the noise of life,
To dance within rhythms, I feel so rife.

It's not just knowledge I seek to expand,
But emotional and spiritual awakening,
Exploring new dimensions of thought,
Feeling, connection—lessons taught.

A butterfly, in beauty and height, it soars,
Far above its caterpillar form.
Does it remember how it crawled,
Or in earth-bound toil, did it dream of flight?

Where does my metamorphosis lead?
Is it like a butterfly born?
Is this why each stage must be endured,
Living as fully as one can?

Like the butterfly, I wonder where I'm led—
Will I transform or fade instead?
Am I truly losing my way?

Should I have spent more time in the now,
Not always worried about the how?
Or have I chased after tasks, blind to my soul,
And missed the moments that made me whole?

All I think about is what I have done,
And not enough about who I have become.

Acceptance of Mortality

Coming to terms with mortality is perhaps the most profound form of acceptance. It's about recognizing the finite nature of our existence and making peace with it. This form of acceptance is not about despair but about finding meaning in the time we have left.

In "Why I Travel with Terminal Cancer," I write about how facing mortality has reshaped my perspective on life. This poem is an ode to living fully, even when time feels limited, and finding meaning in the act of living itself.

> *"I travel not just for myself,*
> *But to inspire somebody else—*
> *To show there's more beyond despair,*
> *More than just the couch, the chair."*

This stanza captures what it's all about: the understanding that while we all face mortality, how we choose to live in the meantime makes all the difference. We all die—I just know that mine will occur sooner than I had hoped. But in this awareness, I've found a deeper commitment to living fully. I want people to realize that we all have choices in how we live our lives. For me, life isn't about residing on a couch; it's about feeling the wind toss my hair, the cold spray of the ocean drench me, the warmth of the sun on my skin, and the hoot of an owl in the night.

Thom Barrett

Why I Travel with Terminal Cancer

Travel has always called my name,
A way to push my body's frame,
To touch the world, to feel alive,
In nature's arms, I used to thrive.

But now, with stage IV cancer's weight,
My journeys hold a different fate.
It's not the scenery alone I seek,
But life itself, in moments, is sweet.

Each ticket booked, each bag I pack,
It feels like a step in taking back.
The parts of me I thought were gone,
But still, they stir, still carry on.

I watched my grip on life grow weak,
Like water slipping from my reach.
Yet travel gives me power anew,
To choose the path that I pursue.

I travel not just for myself,
But to inspire somebody else—
To show there's more beyond despair,
More than just the couch, the chair.

It would be easy to sit and wait,
Let illness shape the final state.
But I refuse to give it reign,
So I board the next flight again.

Defying cancer's cruel design,
Each mountain trekked, each stroke of mine,
Marks out a line that illness can't erase—
A bold rebellion, a fierce embrace.

I keep moving, I keep trying,
Refusing still to stop flying.
I want others in my place,
To find their strength, to seek, to race.

Travel, too, connects my heart,
With those I love, though we may part.
In Antelope's golden light, I stand,
With bison roaming through the land.

Or watching Yellowstone's icy plume,
With daughters near, the cold consumed.
These moments last beyond my time,
They stay with me; they feel sublime.

And when they speak of who I was,
I hope it's more than illness's claws.
Not a man frail, bound to bed,
But one who lived, who dared instead.

I hope they see me on the sea,
Dodging icebergs, wild and free.
These are the tales I leave behind,
Of journeys bold and unconfined.

Vulnerability's no sign of weak,
It's strength to show the truths I speak.
And so, I write, and so I roam,
Hoping others find their home.

Mother Nature gives me peace,
In mountains high and rivers' crease.
Her rhythms constant, her spirit grand,
Despite the marks of a human hand.

I stand on summits, cold winds bite,
And watch the sun fade out of sight.
In those vast peaks, I see my place,
Small yet alive, in nature's grace.

Illness shows that life is frail,
But travel sets my spirit's sail.
In new horizons, I find the now—
The only thing I can allow.

The Strength of Surrender

On beaches soft, with waves that play,
The salt and sun melt time away.
No illness here, no fear, no doubt,
Just simple joy in life's layout.

As I face mortality's door,
I still seek life; I still want more.
In different cultures, people, lands,
I find a sense of something grand.

So let me wander, let me roam,
In every place, I find my home.
For in the time I still have left,
Each laugh, each step, is my own gift.

I write my ending, line by line,
With beauty, love, and hope entwined.
And more than this, I want to show—
Even in pain, we still can grow.

Even in the hardest fight,
We all still have the will to light,
Our way through the darkness, choose to live—
There's still so much the world can give.

Freedom in Acceptance

I believe that a significant benefit from acceptance is freedom—freedom from the need to control everything, from resisting life's uncertainties and hardships. It's the understanding that true freedom comes from embracing life as it is, with all its imperfections. While the journey is not over, acceptance is a constant process that is never really over. In this journey of acceptance, I have found that there are other actions that one must take, one of which is choosing joy. Of all the emotions, sorrow, fear, grief, and even happiness, joy is an emotion that we choose to pursue. These other emotions are a result of an event – usually out of our control.

Now, I know that freedom doesn't mean a life without storms. It means being present, appreciating life's simple details—a sunbeam through the window, the warmth of a friend's touch—and choosing to be alive in those moments. Acceptance planted the seeds, and now, freedom blooms where it was nurtured.

Freedom's Path

"Freedom's Path" is the culmination of my journey of acceptance—a journey marked by learning to confront uncertainty, endure adversity, embrace change, and rely on the strength of connection and support. This poem is a reflection of how I came to understand that true freedom isn't an external state or an endless array of choices but an inner peace that emerges when I accept life as it is.

My Journey of Acceptance

To find the freedom that we seek,
We must accept the truths that speak—
Of life's uncertain, shifting sands,
And futures cupped in fragile hands.

Acceptance of Self-Reflection

When mirrors show the soul's refrain,
We look within to confront the pain.
In knowing who we truly are,
We light our path and become our star.
Released from judgment, we begin,
To live with truth beneath our skin.

Acceptance of Support

To lean on others, heart exposed,
Is where the quiet hope is posed.
A trembling hand, a gentle nod,
Reminds us we are not just flawed.
We find in others' warmth and touch,
A freedom that we need so much—
Freedom from the ache of alone,
From battles we thought we'd fight on our own.
Freedom from judgment's heavy weight,
From needing to seem strong and great.
Freedom to grieve, to laugh, to cry,
To ask for solace, to wonder why.
In others' care, in kindness shared,
We're free to feel valued, to feel repaired.

Acceptance of Emotional Responses

To feel the depths, both joy and fear,
To shed the weight of every tear.
Emotions ebb, emotions flow,
They shape us, teach us, help us grow.
No longer bound by shame or strife,
We let them pass, and breathe new life.

Acceptance of Loss and Limitations

The loss we bear, the lines we trace,
Define the edges of our space.
Yet in these bounds, a world appears,
A canvas formed by hopes and tears.
When strength is found in what remains,
We walk through life unbound by chains.

Acceptance of Change and Transformation

The tides of change will sweep and churn,
And strip us bare where we might yearn.
But fighting waves yields bitter cost,
While riding them, we find what's lost.
Acceptance lets us shape our sail,
To navigate each shifting gale.

Acceptance of Adversity

When hardship casts its shadow long,
We gather strength, grow tough, grow strong.
Not yielding in defeat's embrace,
But learning from each battered trace.
With courage, scars become a guide—
A map of where we've bled and survived.

Acceptance of Uncertainty

It starts when doubt is faced, not fought,
When questions halt, no answers bought.
In letting go of what may be,
We plant the seeds of being free.
No longer bound by rigid schemes,
We live within the day's own dreams.

Acceptance of Mortality

Thus, freedom comes, not wild, unbound,
But subtle, sacred, and newly found.

The Strength of Surrender

To wake each morning, choose to be,
Alive, aware, in harmony.
It's not the grasp of endless choice,
But steady heart and steady voice.

Freedom in Acceptance

The ache remains, as does the storm,
Yet joy can dance where grief was born.
In small details, in fleeting smiles,
Freedom rests in simple trials.
Not needing control nor asking why,
Just being here, beneath the sky.
The power to live, to hope, to weave,
A life of meaning, though we grieve.
Acceptance sows a mighty seed,
And freedom blooms where it is freed.

Conclusion

Acceptance is not a place I arrived at but a practice I embraced. In the unfolding of my life—through adventures across landscapes and through the inner valleys of grief, change, and uncertainty—I learned that acceptance is as layered as the snowfields I once skied and as enduring as the mountains that watched over me.

This journey has shown me that acceptance begins not with a grand declaration but with small, daily acts. It's in the quiet surrender to what I cannot change and the active decision to find joy in what remains. It's in recognizing that sorrow and joy can coexist, that grief does not cancel out love, and that living fully means allowing space for both.

I once believed that strength was in defiance, in proving myself capable against life's harshest trials. But I came to understand that strength lies equally in allowing, in choosing to show up even when the outcome is uncertain, and in finding joy as a conscious act of will. In choosing joy, we find resilience—a quiet strength that sustains us through life's storms.

To choose joy is to say, "I am here, in this moment, and I choose to see the light." It's watching the morning sun filter through trees, feeling gratitude for the breath in my lungs, or smiling at the warmth of a shared memory.

Freedom is not a destination to be reached, nor is it something granted by external circumstances. Instead, freedom is an experience that unfolds as we walk the path of acceptance. It is discovered not to deny life's truths but to embrace them—our emotions, our limitations, and the uncertainties of existence.

Through acceptance, we release the weight of resistance and find peace within the moments we are given. This journey is not about triumphing over life's challenges but about living fully alongside them. In this, we find liberation—not as an endpoint but as a profound and ongoing source of strength, clarity, and grace.

As this final poem reflects, freedom is born in the act of letting go, surrendering to what is, and choosing to live with openness and intention.

It reminds us that even amidst life's complexity, we have the power to shape our experience and find meaning in the present moment.

So, I leave you with this final reflection: a reminder that acceptance is not a single act but a lifelong path—one where freedom is discovered, step by step, within its embrace.

Thom Barrett

Freedom Within Acceptance

To accept is not to yield or fall,
But to rise within life's call.
The tides may shift, the winds may roar,
Yet we find strength on every shore.
It's in the letting go of strife,
That we unearth the roots of life.
A quiet grace, a steady hand,
Guides us through this fragile land.
Freedom blooms within the flow,
As truths unfold, as burdens go.
Each breath, each tear, a gentle guide,
Revealing peace where fears reside.
Not in control, but in the stream,
We glimpse the freedom in life's scheme.
Acceptance whispers, soft yet true,
"Freedom is here—it lives in you."

A Note of Gratitude

Thank you for joining me on this journey through The Strength of Surrender. Writing this book has been a deeply personal and transformative experience, and I hope it has offered you insight, inspiration, or simply a moment of connection.

As you close these pages, I hope you take with you a reminder that acceptance and joy are not just choices we make once, but choices we make repeatedly. They are acts of courage that light our way forward. Whatever journey you find yourself on, may you embrace each moment with an open heart, knowing that even in the face of uncertainty, there is freedom to be found.

Acceptance, after all, is the path we walk. Joy is the light that guides us along it.

If this book has moved you or resonated with you in any way, I would be truly grateful if you would take a moment to leave a review. Your feedback not only helps me grow as an author but also ensures that this book can reach others who might find it meaningful.

In today's world, reviews are a powerful way to share stories and ideas with a wider audience. Whether you leave a review on Amazon or on my website at www.livinglifewhiledying.com, your thoughts will help amplify this message of acceptance and freedom.

Thank you for your time, your reflection, and your willingness to explore these pages with me.

With gratitude,
Thom Barrett

Acknowledgments

My journey has been anything but smooth—a road filled with challenges, potholes, and steep cliffs. Yet, the support of others has made it not only navigable but meaningful.

To Steve and Joyce, Mike and Mary—your friendship has been a constant source of strength and joy along this path.

To Jamie, thank you for your unwavering dedication in helping me unwittingly craft this book. Your ability to keep us grounded, even when distractions beckoned, has been invaluable.

To my brother John and his son Troy, your support in handling the daily life chores has been a gift beyond measure. By lightening my load, you've allowed me to focus on the passions that bring purpose to my life. And most of all, to Annika—your love and support have been my compass, my shelter, and my reason to keep moving forward. Without you, this road would be impassable.

To each of you, my deepest gratitude. You've not only helped me navigate the journey but have made it one worth traveling.

About the Author

Thom, a former PwC partner with an impressive 35-year tenure, has always been driven by a relentless sense of adventure. Now retired and living in Cape Cod, he spends his summers crafting custom furniture in his workshop and the rest of the year exploring new horizons with his loyal companion, Dexter.

Thom's explorations have taken him across Europe, North America, and, more recently, throughout South America and Antarctica. Thom's future plans are equally ambitious, aiming to experience the wonders of the Arctic as he embarks on a two-month breathtaking journey from Iceland's geothermal wonders and glacial beauty to Greenland's rugged ice fjords and Inuit culture. He will then sail through Canada's legendary Northwest Passage, encountering wildlife and Inuit communities, and conclude in a serene fishing village like Tuktoyaktuk in the Northwest Territories, where Arctic landscapes and vibrant local culture create an unforgettable finale.

Whether navigating rugged backcountry trails or embracing the vibrant cultures of remote Arctic communities, Thom's journeys reflect his boundless curiosity and love for life's wild beauty.

Amidst his adventures, Thom has been courageously battling incurable stage IV cancer for eight years. While the diagnosis is considered terminal, he continues to live fully, viewing each day as an opportunity to inspire others. Thom's journey is about more than his own experiences—it's a heartfelt reminder to cherish every moment, whether navigating a personal cancer journey or supporting a loved one.

Thom has authored several books that reflect his unique perspective on life:

Living While Dying:
My Cancer Journey

Chasing My Northern Lights:
Traveling Life's Unpredictable Road Where Adventure and Introspection Blur

Embrace the Cold:
A Guide to Solo Winter Travel and Backcountry Survival

Between Worlds:
The Duality of Living and Letting Go

Dear Readers,

As you journey through *The Strength of Surrender*, I hope this chapbook has resonated with you and provided solace on your path to acceptance and joy. My experiences with grief, vulnerability, and the beauty of surrender have shaped these poems, offering insights into navigating life's challenges with resilience.

To deepen your understanding and connection, I invite you to visit my website: www.livinglifewhiledying.com. Here, you'll find additional resources, reflective prompts, and a supportive community dedicated to embracing life's complexities and celebrating moments of joy.

For daily inspiration and updates on my writing journey, follow me on Instagram at @Thom.Barrett. Let's connect and share our stories as we navigate the intricacies of life together, discovering the strength that comes from surrender and the joy found in acceptance.

With warmth,
Thom

www.ingramcontent.com/pod-product-compliance
Lightning Source LLC
Chambersburg PA
CBHW050517100526
44581CB00001B/4